CROSSLIGHT FOR YOUNGBIRD

ASIYA WADUD

CROSSLIGHT FOR
YOUNGBIRD

Nightboat Books
New York

ISBN 978-1-937658-87-8

Design and typesetting by HR Hegnauer
Text set in Bembo Standard
Cover art: "A Good Timing" by Ping Zheng. Oil Sticks on Paper, 18" x 24."
Courtesy of the artist.

Cataloging-in-publication data is available from the Library of Congress

Nightboat Books
New York
www.nightboat.org

PART I
northern wheatear see water

PART II
salt carrion constellation

PART I

northern wheatear see water

...and either I'm nobody, or I'm a nation
Derek Walcott, *The Schooner Flight*

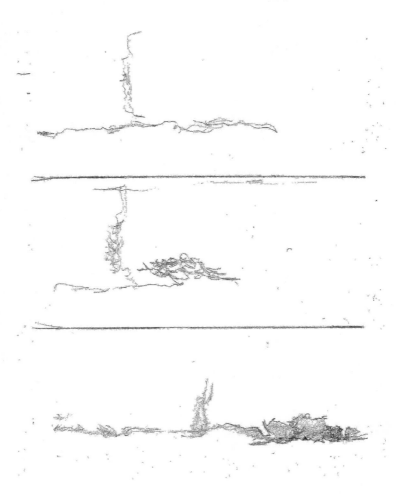

home 16 ways

In Swahili ndege means bird and airplane, intertwined. En a new patois ndege significa pajaro na Flugzeug.

To speak of a young bird is to say nothing of its boomerang comeback. Let alone its able wings. Let alone its constitution. And of its webbed feet as metronome. And eyes a gilded staid light. And gaped golden teeth. And tongue a ready supplicant. Small body roundly racked with pain. Who keeps watch through these thickets, young bird? To speak of a young bird is to say nothing of its glistening plumage. And nothing of its matted plumage. And nothing of its missing plumage. Whose downy feathers know no borders. Whose supple mind learns mother tongues? Whose strong jaws to claim the sounds? Say Amira. Amira. Say Fatima. Fatima. Say Mustafa. Mustafa. Say pillage. And Mash'allah. For the storm. That's come and gone. Young bird fed from birth. Bismillah calca make da bone firm. Bismillah many ways to call a home. Bismillah a bevy beats, syncopated — with our gangster country we always love.

And in any language it's the same: bird is airplane, intertwined. The ascendant. The ancients. The son. The waters. That swell. That keep. The anchor. So urgent. Won't burnish or shank my home. And if it does there are 15 new ways to say home

Keleti. Lampedusa. Calais. Quietude. Mash'allah. Hamburg. Patera. Skorskog. A sovereign nation's peace flag. And 16 ways to say home. After home is a bounty. After home is wrought in name alone. And after it's a new shame. A savage pummeling at the Balkan border. Young bird, wings relent. But Mash'allah always: a crisp, clean shrift.

Newbird, you will find the air here easier on your two lungs. You will see some searching eyes. Some webbed feet as metronome, other tongues other supplicants. Know most untamed birds come in peace and just a few to feast on carrion. Everybird has a God. Everybird has a compass in its brain. Young bird, your plumage is coming in full, velveteen, shirking doom. We're lucky. Sisi ni bahati. Our fortune. Insh'allah. The will. The ascendant.

Lida meet lorry
after Parndorf

Her name was Lida. From the family of Rahm. Someone loved the baby and boarded her on a northbound lorry. They began their journey in Röszke. Revved the engine maybe, standing room only, undoubtedly. The man at the wheel, Mitko, I wonder where he keeps his own humanity. Tucked in a hull abut his neat steady breathing. Maybe a wallet photo of his own mother to remind him he's still breathing. Shame he won't extend outstretched to the 71 asphyxiating.

Imagine for a minute the calm sure that bade them. Slick near the edges but a near god to keep them. Mothers outstretched. Arms that cupped them. Teeth that made the pleading sound, reunion. Heavy tongue envelop them. Papers that name them. Maybe Aamir. Maybe Hassan. Maybe empire. Maybe break back. And some the red sun. And among them those who bade the quick waters. Lida speaking. Her toddler brother underwing. Lida clenching for small air, just enough for a baby. Just enough to claim victory.

Mitko, 29, behind the wheel. What did he ever think of his mother? His own unflailing breathing? Mitko, you think he knows of Lida's failing ventricles? Of the shrift her father unfolds? Her name was Lida. From the family of Rahm. Someone loved the baby.

Now a container holds the bodies of the 71. They were all once breathing. Among them the able ventricles. Among them capacious atria. They were all named at birth. They were named on the day they were born. They were anticipated. Among them there were a likely many eyes. Some who loved the sun. Some the red earth. Some the green on which they cut their teeth. Some black forest. Each yearn their own yearn. Each mourn their own mourn. Each fought their own won. Everyone with some kin before them.

Didn't they all know the world as it was named? Bits of clothes, 17 travel documents. 40 cell phones. In a meat truck. In which the cooling system had been shut. In which the air ducts were blocked. In which god sepulchers light? What kind of rancor? The derelict is how they die. What kind of god won't see them? What kind of man drives a truck across the border forgetting his own mother? With each breath Mitko took could he not then name them? Name the diminished breaths of the 71? With each breath Mitko took could he not remember in his lorry some who loved the sun? Some like Lida who maybe yet to know the sun? Some like her toddler brother dying to show her the sun? Some like her mother who always seeks out the supple sun.

They began their journey in Röszke. Mitko, 29, behind the wheel. What did he ever think of his mother? His fissure of humanity? You think he knows of Lida's ventricles and atria, newborn heart the size of ripe walnut? Postage stamp the size of a loved beating heart. Of contours. Of countries. Of lorries.

You can say their names. They were named. Some mother. Some father, pushed the baby into the waiting new world.

Some mother gripped the yolk sack between her teeth. Some father held the baby just the length of his musculature. Eyes glisten for this one, alive. Make to see life. And then name them. Maybe in their likeness. Maybe in earnest. Maybe to capture the fold. Maybe as a reaching. Maybe to know the baby came. And now 71 asphyxiating. In the end they know somebody still loved them? In the end they know they walk slick near the edges? They know others came before them? They remember their mothers' mouths gripped them? The disavowed. The vulgar. The sun moored. The failed marooned. The god come lately. The black sinister. The widow that grips tightlock the seal. The body in a state of repose. The body as it depreciates. The body at the end composed. Lida is a baby loved enough to bring on a lorry. From the family of Rahm. Someone loved the baby and boarded her on a northbound lorry.

Some latitude. A crease.

A double exposure as backdrop: *frame 1*: Amagansett Beach, gentlest waves crest foamy, wash up emerald kelp and muted black scalloped shells. *frame 2*: a long exposure of the old Jewish Hospital, the long light of the toy camera illuminating what we can not see.

Rilke's "Widening Circles" as a scaffold — first stanza at the beginning and second stanza at the end

I live my life in widening circles
that reach out across the world.
I may not complete this last one
but I give myself to it.

Repeat, to incant [whisper]: "I may not complete this last one but I give myself to it"
Overlay unfinished poem [don't whisper]: Peter, I think in you. A litany is a stark plain, a cleansing newness, a buffered passage, a litany is a low tide, a heat embalmed by wolves aeternam and you are just one.

Low tide washes up a young clam family. We pocket a few shells to remember their mercurial lives. A salted mist licks me from the ocean while the sun breaks overhead. The dunes roll, the sun licks too. Many people are among the dunes but from our vantage we see only infinite, listing, unkempt hills and a demure, keen red–black fox.

The warm, clear assuredness of a hachiya persimmon tree vibrating in its own radiance in the dead middle of December — a middle earth hewn amber glow. The globes stoke their own flame.

A field of variegated greens. Requiem æternam dona eis, Domine, et lux perpetua luceat eis. Luceat eis.

A dinghy is a lifeboat, moored. 3,771 lives lost in the Mediterranean in 2015. A patera is a lifeboat, moored. At its narrowest, the Strait of Gibraltar is 14 kilometers across.

I think with each variegated leaf, the new variegation lends some knowledge, a palimpsest marking some memory. Some latitude. A crease. The variegation tells a story replete. I drape the pothos over my arm and know they, too, must have done the same to the same leaf somewhere along.

I circle around God, around the primordial tower.
I've been circling for thousands of years
and I still don't know: am I a falcon,
a storm, or a great song?

conversations from empire

Omar:

I am a good swimmer, I've always lived by the sea. I am a good swimmer, I've always lived by the sea. I set out on this journey, it has not been easy. The rocks at Rhodes nearly ran us aground. The doors to the hull, they keep them locked. There is water on all sides but not much for drinking. The gangs they chase us even on the high seas. Bismillah from Mogadishu. And I am a good swimmer, I've always loved the sea. The way its light envelops me. And the manner that it holds my dreams. And the tides that mark each new moon. And the children who wash up with the tide. And the seals who incant young doom. And how the salted seas preserve a dream. And the doors to the hull, they keep them locked. And the Mare Nostrum guard their seas. And their rubber bullets pocked my brother. But the long arm of empire, it grips back and we arrive on rotten pallets.

Now, we are but arm's length from rescue. And we all need some grace from God. This journey has not been easy. The light of the search vessel it beckons and we 700 rush starboard. And our weight lumbers and our vessel topples. Now, I have always loved the sea. I save whom I can. A baby be damned without a mother. A mother be damned without her child. A man be damned without a country. A country be damned without a people. A nation of no one trickle north and the long arm of empire it whips back. I am a good swimmer. I've always loved the sea.

Martin:

On April 11, 1945 the 6th US Armored Division liberated Buchenwald. Infantrymen came with their K-Rations: meat, cheese, biscuits. A body after handed years of starkest deprivation must go easy. Some newly freed ate their ration unrelentingly, who can blame them? Remembering a taste for cheese and meats the richness of being free. Now I have always loved being free. To taste it so keenly. Many perished in early April when their bodies could not consume these markers of being free. What is a body if not one that learns to live through darkest depravity?

What kind of God licks back like that? What kind of ire washes up the hungry to be free? What dark horse come to greet when a mare seek her baby? Why the empire licks and we have to lick back?

Well, Omar, let us break bread for our brethren. For the baby be damned without a mother, for the mother be damned without her child, for the man be damned without a country. For the God who take some seeming no reason. So close to liberation and some empire licks back.

collage for Youngbird

after Malia Wollan's "How To Hold a Heart"

a heart has four chambers:
upper left ventricle
upper right ventricle
and lower left atria
lower right atria
a year some places has four seasons
we call them by different names
in different languages
of her country Youngbird says
there's only one way to hold a beating heart
the heart is a muscle
that warms to any country
neatly nesting like a retreating army
beat back as the day's selfish sun
and swiftly swaddled and saved for loving
always cradle a heart in two hands: so it remembers
when it had a mother
this is how to hold a beating heart:
slide your hand behind the heart until your knuckles
graze the smooth
the heart is pink noise that fits inside a mitten
hold its soft warm animal in your hand
hold the hot animus in your palm
take a scalpel to the cleanest piece
and tuck it underwing
know that most us just carry on. know in my little

knapsack I carry a heart and Youngbird's able lungs
the heart is a muscle
that warms to any country
these days I count my country some:
the longing for an upper left ventricle
but I ably subsist on my atria
bird can feed bird
when dearth abuts the sun

Youngbird, highwaterhome

I was born poor and black just below the Mason-Dixon line where a just God justified all my light inside. To mean I was born in Washington. All my life somebody say, where are you from as if this was never my country. What of my forefathers who roundly paid for me, they broke their back for the Uzzells of Greene County. I count Caldonia, Rebecca, Cy and so many kin their backs table top back five generations. What you see in me and don't see the same country? What in my face don't say English mother tongue. What you see and don't see slave marooned? What at seven I'm dying for a sliver of country. And my mother says this country never gave us anything. Pledge allegiance to any nation's flag, our kinship be damned. You want some country just count your brethren. At 9 I start writing letters to girls across my country eke out some curve of a sovereign nation and the bevy of letters becomes the world: Joburg, Vienna, Manila, Accra, Milan, Lima to Tokyo troubling some country festooned with sun — when a country doesn't claim you, just gather your own.

And I learn early a country can never be claimed. Because if someone won't see you they won't see you just the same. And in small imagination they see just two ways to be black. Never stay in a place with such a small mind because you criminal or slave both the outcome the same.

Now I was born poor and black just below the Mason-Dixon line where a just God justified all my light inside. Now, I know I am free. I know the difference between a dinghy and a refugee. I know my family broke their backs table top whipped black lacerated Middle Passage Southern sun burn direct.

In the south of Spain I was once 21 passport shanked from under me. I spent Christmas Day in the shadows. My only papers my own mouth incant my Middle Passage route. Those weeks I never been so alone without some kin without some country snow capped bone chill Melilla black African. But I yearn aspiration for a nation's flag. And black Africans in my town say where you from? Dakar? Ouagadougou? Cameroon? My brothers, no, I'm lineage of slave marooned. I always remember I am free. But these weeks were hopeful when Dakar and Mali and Cameroon claimed me.

I was born poor and black just below the Mason–Dixon line where a just God justified all my light inside. In Bed Stuy French tourists come at me, a bit I understand but can never speak. But I see an empire's subtleties. Stranger, please. Grant me my own story to come with a country. And don't be so sure the river flows downstream. Truth be we maybe all long for the same long. All and seek a sturdy highwaterhome. I love a country and warm to most borders. I love a country that abuts some sun. Me, I'm just free. And anyway, know a country's levee will always breech a border. So pass through a ready sieve some what you need to make a little country by the supple, giving sea.

Calais, onward

empire wrought boundless
mollusked isle full light
moored light come light
a sepulcher if not
mark a journey supplicate
pray mohammed
and fatima
pray amira
and insh'allah
a litany
of all the names
of all the men
the women. all
our progeny
every chaos every need
our best maps
what mattered what became
a book of prayers
saved for daylight
and moonlight
and damned light
to retrieve a body
all. these days
we remembered
to make it, to mourn
to mark a journey
a white shrift unsullied

mash'allah my god
can deliver my god
saves face my god
solemn hunter my god
a privation my god
in the light call it, pilgrimage
call it crystalline, call it
empire call it
salt honed call it
calais onward
london

still life on lesbos

I would not think to touch the sky with two arms
—Sappho, *If Not, Winter: Fragments of Sappho*
translated by Anne Carson

imagine sappho fishing for her
meager supper
imagine sappho as a clam
sappho mercurial
staying lit by the rubbish pyre
imagine sappho doubling down on
an uncertain patera
imagine sappho in a life vest no love
imagine sappho with bunions heel
spurs and hammertoe imagine sappho in
a diving bell port starboard lesbos
imagine sappho as the sun
expect the sun to run aground
now see the sun luminous
now see it when we had some
see the many eels that will carry us
pray the life immemorial
pray the life at high noon
a sealed edge our religion
imagine sappho mopping the camp's floors
imagine sappho still liminal

awaiting her mother's remittance
sappho at the end resettled in hamburg
now touch the sky with two arms
now touch the sky with two arms

I. Fittja, Sweden

the Fibonacci catacombs of my one neighbor's sunflower
and the new patois of English–Swedish–Spanish
the few families resettled in Fittja's towers
an Arctic journey, a sun eclipses Skorskog
a soundless archipelago, who is the patron saint of fjords?
and where was his family during the war?
not every hamlet had a patron saint or hero

II. Strait of Gibraltar

the only one rescued from a capsized vessel
and the sure fist that meets you
demanding to be named

III. The Balkan route

in Swahili ndege means 'bird' and 'airplane',
intertwined. the final heartbeat, some hopes laid bare
some errant hairs that occasionally shelter me
my kitten's catch caught in the day's final ray

IV. Keleti Station, Budapest

Insh'allah, my patron saint for refuge
the watchmen I'm certain are guiding
us aground towards the day's
loveless doomed sky
Keleti meets fickle border
abutting the winter's first
neat direct hues

remember: we, too, are but the fold
a struggle to reach the Astral

All can be considered light when you name it light. All light refracted is a hopeful light. A life raft carries the bodies of the just now dead. All hope descends to cloak a finality. The finality reveres a moon's recent perigee. And the perigee speaks of a featherweight doom. The apogee speaks of the deadweight in vague terms. Rather preferring the swath of even a cool northern light. The north is but a dedicated orientation. The north is but a detriment. And the underside of a shadow can be the eventual light.

All we carefully assemble becomes our own archipelago: the time that waned when we thought it stood still, the burden and the blessing of an able constitution. Light becomes luminous when you name it light. The most liminal light shirks a dereliction. All light is a desire line. All light begets better light. And assuredly it ekes out its keenest knowledge. Anything is light when it bears it heavy. Anything can be light when you call it light.

All is luminous when the apogee shirks doom. All is luminous when I was seven years old. All is light laid bare when a dinghy reaches the shore. All is laid bare with a dinghy run aground. All is barren when a baby is buried nameless, a headstone simply naming its only reference. All is burnished when an infant reaches shore. And a shadow is the underside of the eventual light.

All light ultimately crests, new light reaches. I assume this is God's will. I assume God's will is ascendant. Light is limitless. A searchlight rightly casts a final glow. The lambent light is its own direct knowing. It's okay: we got this. Remember, we, too, are but the fold. That which is creased ultimately sees its coming nation. All is luminous when the apogee shirks doom. All is luminous when the apogee shirks doom.

The air in here stands still. The air stands still while I read the news. There is but a subtle lick to note the air, the air in here. Once I took the good, able air for granted. Another patera off the coast of lampedusa. The patera's empty oil drum succumbs to the water. Men grip their end from the open air. The air in here rustles a little and the wind moves me. The wind takes me. The air in here? That's a security. The air in here carries a blue passport. Carries stature and status. A strong back and access. Carries kin and a need. And the air holds firm when I forget who it is I wanted to become. I walk to the window and take in the outside.

Across the way is my neighbor's place. Their futon mattress. Their slow measured movements. Their golden living room lights. The quality of the air they breath. Their breaths while they sleep a measured sleep. Whether they wait for a certain season and knowing what that means. If I turn in I see my own life. The one I know and the one in the knowing. The one I have and the one in the making. The fold of my mother. The air here stands still. The air in here is always partly hydrogen. The air in here matters and it supplicates. The air in here is unmade. The air is one part oxygen to a twin hydrogen. lampedusa is a teeny island, a harbor where air is known to stagnate and sometimes casts again luminous light. Drowning is the act of water displacing air in the lungs. I once took the good, able air for granted.

I know how to find a stillness. I know where there could be life. I know to seek out a golden ginkgo. I am pretty peaceable. I consider the air piecemeal. This is a question of naming the unnamed. Of counting four walls towards a scaffolding of light. Of a prostrate heart to eke out some names. Of knowing the air in here is the air that matters. And from this vantage the ginkgo won't always know that behind the stillness is the air that will hold us.

> I'm just a red nigger who love the sea,
> I had a sound colonial education,
> I have Dutch, nigger, and English in me,
> and either I'm nobody, or I'm a nation
> —Derek Walcott, *The Schooner Flight*

Chamber archipelago

Derek Walcott, Tabarca's hewn of salt
barnacles and bambini
windmills spun like sterns and

a salted constellation by which I mean
the sun does not cease and the sun belongs

by which I mean we remember a
changing Mediterranean Sea, angling
for new angles to lap
its north south east west
mistral storm winds, salt flats
hillside stepped vineyards
heat, stars, travelers

as in Lampedusa, the sovereign nation of
we three, eyelids creased, our bodies
strewn asunder our bodies strewn afield

by which I mean there is just
one gravedigger and anyway
we're living, as in we are finally floating
so free bobbing, amniotic

because if we are floating we are
not leeching life because if we are salt
buoyed we
remain collective and we are floating
and finally, staggeringly

God bestows light, Mr. Walcott:
Tabarca's hewn of salt

In light of our disparate anchors

ten we are knowing lapping children
nine and we mew with urgency
both night and day
eight
we have a humble hearty appetite, though
seven are secretly
never sated
six
six of my dearest kin profess a keen yearning
six
against a fickle Balkan border
five
is the color of the affronted night sky
four. borders. each one wracks me
three, I request the salt to alchemize
two — two searchlights, marooned
two: the Strait of Gibraltar narrows
and delivers
one
close
your both
dog eyes
and consider
when

PART II

salt carrion constellation

All the world began with a yes. One molecule
said yes to another molecule, and life was born.
Clarice Lispector, *The Hour of the Star*

young warblers, golden plovers, loons

Doom and resolve each keep their own metronome, a long clear wide shore, some black threadbare jeans slick in the rain, a doe with long lashes, a dog's heartbeat, the metronome now almost syncopated, a lens already focused. Doom is walking on your own two feet towards a clean expanse. Resolve is the ready supplication, a pilgrimage to a church on your knees. Resolve is the rain-hewn path, it glistening high against the black asphalt. Resolve is the needle's eye, with a single way in. Carrion is the twin stench of doom and resolve.

It begins at the steady still waters ninety miles north of New York and a persevering, onward Northern Wheatear carries under its wing the stench of the carp to this desolate dolphin-blue stretch of the Camargue. Here the carrion odor is hypnotic, renders me mute, still, and changed. Here the carrion reigns heavy, reigns down, an end so honed. And the ocean curries solemnity, yes, but there's, too, fraternity in its kin shores. On either end water laps on the edge of the Atlantic, and inevitably western edges come to know their eastern boundaries too. There where the ocean floor is eight kilometers deep, the water's east–west seams meet and fold in on one another, jostle a little, and settle into an undulation. Each wave washes up something new. Sometimes a clam family, an orca fin, a plastic flipper, an amber tinted bottle, more ancient carrion. Something in the sea remarks. The tides come and go and the doom and resolve each keep their own metronome.

The carrion, once tucked into the Northern Wheatear's wing, bobs amniotic making its way from the nebulous Atlantic's outer edge, washing up on the Camargue. In both Milford and in the Camargue and in all places before and after, I search out the sun, which is never far off even when the light casts its dimmest glow, and even at night when the light transmutes into Orion and some other light form: maybe some rings of Saturn, a demure Pluto. Oh there's the sun I will say, pointing at the moon.

* * *

The rain is beating now and a cool calm engulfs me. I hold the resolve and hold the doom too. The sun rises and we are absolved when it eventually sets. Before it sets I want to be propelled on a bicycle to the ocean. And then I ache to lap at the sea.

I was small when I learned that you set out on your surest foot, not stopping until you reach the point. You walk with your little torch and a little heat on your head and don't let up. See a point in the distance? Now go headlong towards it. I carry the bike down four flights of stairs, check the tires for air, pack a pannier with a pear and angle myself towards the sun. I feel to not be alone. I feel to know another little heart cradling my own. I feel to be marsupial. I feel a warmth from my navel to my nape.

It's January 23, 2016. Today the baby would be born, but it is not being born today. I spent June with skeins of wool draped over my legs, knitting the warmest thing next to my skin. In this I would keep the baby warm. From womb to breast from breast to cradle from cradle to grave. I'm so scared to kill my own young. To feast upon my young. To let them suckle. My legs burn hot under the wool. On January 23, New York is pummeled by a snowstorm; it would have buried a newborn.

See a point in the distance? Now ride headlong to it. Don't let up when the sky breaks and only turn back when all the errant, unlikely seams neatly meet.

★   ★   ★

Once we were hungry, I was fifteen she was thirteen and we went wading in the fountain, cuffed our jeans and hunched our backs and made a coin sack for pennies and quarters and

35

dimes and nickels. Quarters first in the natural hierarchy. Once we were hungry and fished for everything.

A few days before that, there are only pennies left in the little glass coin jar. That's the only money in the house. Spread the pennies on the bed and count them out by tens. Sink them into their rolls. Take said rolls to the bank and exchange them for dollars. Order dinner from a dollar menu. See a point in the distance? Now walk, headlong, to it.

★ ★ ★

You cannot compromise with the sun. See the sun? Now see the point in the distance? Now see the point in the distance eclipsed by the sun?

★ ★ ★

I must go all the way to the sea. I'm in serene waters, taking pictures with my toy camera. When I get home, I stitch all the frames together to create a panorama. The boat rocks back and forth, sideways. I miss you.

The baby has no heartbeat. I swallow hard and festoon myself against a sliver of certain doom. Of course the baby has no heartbeat. Little bear, you spent 77 days with your own black thoughts, chasing a scythe, a sickle, a sepulcher, a sentry. You spent all those days chasing your own slippery tail, fishing for carrion.

The heady stench of carrion radiates out and over the water, past the living, past me, a film of salt already clinging to my skin, I run jubilant. My body is strong now, my mind is aflame now, I'm doubting a lot now, I'm cursing myself now. I'm doubling down now. The flamingos are necking me. The loons are calling me. My body is strong now. I send back a long call. Hello. I beckon. I break. I list. I loll. I capitulate. I mourn. I deliberate. I'm tender. I make a list of all the things that can ride the back of a swan. There would be a feral kitten, my sister born at six months, there would be a little mole, a plum, a bucket of berries, a sliver of Montana. A pearl too close to the sun. There would be a supple star.

Doom is the night that does not break at the day's dawn. Resolve is the daylight as it does not cease; the light transfigurates and bends, yes, but the daylight does not break. I hold these fecund twins.

The road is so slick, the asphalt glistens. My mind is clear and clean, stretched long and wide in front of me. My mind is this way always at a precipice. There are a few imminent dangers, always. The road ahead is a narrow little alley, a gully, always. The road is so slick, the asphalt glistens.

The heady, rich stench of carrion radiates out and over the water, past the living, past me, a film of salt already clinging to my skin, the path is straight on. I run. My body is strong now, my mind is aflame now, I'm doubting a lot now, I'm cursing myself now. The flamingos' necks are closing in on me. They serenade the horses. They atone. They incant and remember their vows.

★   ★   ★

We round the bend and there are horses — steady, sturdy incarnates, melancholy lashes. We need to get close to the horses, to peep the migratory birds, to ride the back of a swan. To be at one. Something in the sailing, sometimes in the light. See a point? Now walk straight towards it.

Sometimes when I am lonely I remember that inside me are all my many organs, all fulgurated, drilled, the uninvited excised. They sent me home with snapshots of my ovaries, two images of each one, holes drilled into them to remove the cysts, the endometriosis gripped with little monopolar scissors. I tuck the images into my wallet to remember I have a body with many pocked organs, and my uterus scraped clean and I am wishing to mother warblers, golden plovers, and loons.

my little nothings form a mouth

Feels good kind of to be cold and alone
I'm remembering when I was a newborn
Fresh and feral born head first and nearly jaundiced
Caully frog legged and liminal
Gracious and silken black and fatty at the middle
Cynic and beatific caustic and crushless
Bludgeoned and bruised cats
Animals swaddled and true

I'm alive I'm listing I'm lolling there's a coldness
I'm underwater I'm flailing
I'm a kitten and I'm nursing I'm a cat and I'm birthing
I'm a dog I'm laughing I'm a dog I'm wailing
I'm a moon and I'm waxing I'm a moon and I'm crescent
I'm a night sky and I'm emptied I'm a night sky and I'm lonesome
I'm a blithe noon and I'm peaking I'm a blithe noon and I'm sharp
    toothed
And I'm Mary Jane and a penny loafer
I'm an afro puff and ring around the collar and
I'm a dirty blackwatch uniform I'm a polyester sweater

I'm asleep and didn't dream I didn't dream and won't dream
I'm a young bear and I'm hungry
I'm a young bear and I'm fly fishing
I'm on Route 10 now with Noah
I'm driving east from Alamogordo
I'm beatific and I'm caustic

I'm a lost monarch in Mexico
I'm a hummingbird at altitude
I'm a hummingbird l'chaim
I'm a warmed egg at the womb
I'm a little plucky and droopy
I'm wrapping a banana in my collar
I'm wringing out my underwear I'm inhaling midnight jasmine
I'm scaling low walls I can walk over it's an easy enough challenge
I see a mountain and look south

I kiss my kittens inside their mouths
I eat my kitten's dirty mouth
I grease my kitten's pink mouth
I tickle my kitten's wet snout
I give my kittens mouth to mouth
I nurse my hummingbirds to health
They feast on mangoes they feast from mouths
They walk straight legged prayers at mecca
Prayers to the east I stuff my womb
With a dirty rag I stuff my womb
With my mouth I stuff my womb with all of that: a hummingbird
A kitten a listing jaundiced frog legged water logged blackness
I shut it off I weld the door I don't look back
I swan dive

Feels good kind of alone and cold
I'm remembering when I was a newborn
Fresh and feral born head first silken black and fatty
At the middle slice of fatback tobacco fields
Stuttering and ugly

God's image and likeness
My mother's maiden my father's refuse
My little nothings form a mouth

Jamila

Most the year there are two cats we have a house
There are three bedrooms no furniture just brown carpet
You sink featherweight cats chase a noon sun freshkills
Fibonacci sunflowers honeybees' catacombs

Most the year there are two cats, funereal
Limitless Jamilas, kittens' names
I'll never know, just the stolid matriarch
Of all Jamilas. On Labor Day 1991 two cats
Birthed fifteen kitten kin combined, all survived. I dipped their
Silken caully heads into my mouth and transmute a Eucharistic
Spes unica, spes unica, spes unica succumb, take their
Mews into my mouth, smother comfort their new world calls

The kittens' slat eyes open, we send them out, each time
One Jamila passes another forms from the ash
Jamila as moored light Jamila as metronome Jamila ancient
Gaped childhood wild, Jamila as arbiter and mother
Quell a doomiest hapless truth as the others retreat
Restless though assured: from this another comes

testament, a litany for many voices

Voices:
GOD: alternately rancor and love
ALL: reciprocated rancor, the greenest pastures, embodied doubt
SOLO: shirked, embodied doubt, reluctant belief

ALL

       God berates fulfilled begets my child bearer of
       unconditional love God is nigh
       God beguiles and betrays grants hope then dismays
       nary a heartbeat in heaven nor blue sky

       Heaven clatters and claims all my names God
       unchained is merciful tonight by and by
       No harbor no beacon God's silent when he's
       speaking, unfettered and too far from home

       God unmoors and upends seeking vengeance for sins
       and a promise shirked mirthless grins
       God breaks my bones keeps leading me home takes
       every last one of these hopes

       God chokes broken mantras impotent and
       unimportant drone of 'what will be will be'.
       God shirks then shames too prideful to name all the
       ways he has left me adrift

What will be will be, impotent and unimportant,
unmoored and unforgotten,
ceaseless and restless this testament

SOLO

God throws rocks sacrilege and rot
Reigning bilious, bereft

SOLO

God gifts a till–less lot

GOD

He is, he is not
All is love, all will not

SOLO

God betrothes a deep rancor

GOD

He is, he is not

SOLO

God waltzes with a derelict dancer

GOD

He is, he is not

SOLO

God tends the greenest pastures

GOD

He is, he is not

SOLO

God is love

GOD

He is, he is not

SOLO

God betrays his lot

GOD

He will not, he will not

SOLO

God equivocates for eight weeks, deliberates indecisive
heartbeat then heartbreak, all my names
All is
All are not
God is not

God sends his prophets and saints to do what he
can't,
calling us by our first names
God is not

ALL

What will be will be, impotent and unimportant,
unmoored and unforgotten,
ceaseless and restless this testament

SOLO

God's deepest belief is to be
Boundless, capacious
Yet he's careless and capricious
And he is volatile and violent
And he is blasphemous and unkind
But God is trying

God is nigh in the night when the stinking dreams of
history hammer, convening at the dawn of this hour

God remembers, reveres, reverses, steers us to the
path with the brightest light

ALL

> And this is the prayer I need to believe
> This is the prayer I need to believe
> This is the prayer I need to believe
> This is the prayer I believe

GOD

> God's eyes downward cast
> God's bent back
> God's hauling his albatross wings in a rucksack
> But God bring us back

SOLO

> We believe what we will believe

GOD

> God comes to us as a man

SOLO

> We learn to love what we cannot see

GOD

> God loves when he can

SOLO

> We live to be what will be will be

ALL

> God understands

ALL

> God's deepest belief is to be honest and free
> Omniscient and observant
> Omnipresent and omnipotent

SOLO

> All love?

GOD

> All is love

SOLO

This is love?

GOD

This is love

SOLO

All is love?

SOLO

We are required to suspend disbelief
Refute skipped beats heartbeats deadbeats
Which at 8 weeks are just webbed feet

SOLO

This is a meditation on god and loss
A mediation on faith forlorn
A sea wall fortifying and strong
A flood of limitless love
This is a fallow field
This is a barren desert
This is a hot wildfire
Extinguished by limitless love

This is a bevy oh my hope
This is a mountain of faith
This is a window and
This is a door
Buoyed by limitless love

This is a rock
This is the valley
the canyon
the fissure

this is the peak
This is belief when it's strong
Grounded in limitless love

God is above
God is above
Oh my son
My love

ALL

This is a testament to what will be will be, impotent
and unimportant, unmoored and unforgotten,
ceaseless and restless this testament

SOLO

These are the little fingers which at eight weeks
Number ten
These are twelve inches of small intestines
These are the fingernails, thin as onionskin
These are eyes and now eyelids

ALL

This is the heartbeat
This is the heartbeat
This is a heartbeat

But this is not a child
But this is not a life
And this is not a future
And this is what I willed
This is what you already know

ALL

> No use in why
> No redemption in why
> No newness in knowing why
> No sleep no rest in why

GOD

> No nothing in why

SOLO

> God knows never is enough
> God peels back the skin
> God breaks our hearts
> While he stabs our backs
> God doesn't always win
>
> God's heart is a fickle hunter
> God's heart is a burning ember
> God's heart is a dry creek
> God's heart is a tumbleweave
>
> And

ALL

> Our love is enduring
> Our love is a bridge
> And
> Our love is a canyon
> Our love is bound and boundless
>
> Still

SOLO

> We believe what we will believe
> God comes to us as a man
> We learn to love what we cannot see
> God loves when he can
> We live to be what will be will be
> God understands
>
> God grows rancid, life leeching
> And longs for oxygen, my brethren,
> God washes up on distant shores fetid, full of stink
> Penitent
>
> We are bobbing in an amniotic sea
> We are all ancient mariners
> And we have our wings
>
> God wakes us in the throes of our worst dreams
> God hears us cry out in a mid-July heat
> God carries us back from sea
> God wakes us from sleep
> God gives us our wings and carries us back
> God is like that
> When he pulls the knife from our back

ALL

> There is the primitive power in speaking
> A perfect purity
> A nod to the infinite possibilities
> A new clarity
> A crisp, cogent understanding

A release of uncertainty
Behind the sea wall consuming me

But decades-old prayers don't fortify a foundry
Cannot be a foundation

Belief is never wholly concrete never complete
Ephemeral always doubting replete and wrangling to
be free
Always a window and a door
Belief

Faith is nearly the hope, this ancient backbone
Faith in prayers and mantras of what will be will be,
but

Faith is a windowless sanctuary
Faith is a bludgeoned belief
Faith is a promise to the unseen and
Faith is a rotting dream

ALL

But take shelter in knowing that
God always beckons back
God always look back

This is a door
This is a window
This is a thing on my back

God doesn't look back

Same gods, new sins
Big gods, small men

This is a door
This is a window
This is a thing on my back

God can't look back

Same gods, new sins
Big gods, small men

This is the door
This is the window
This is the thing on my back

Same gods, new sins
Big gods, small men
Same gods, new hope

a supplication

take this: meager paltry offerings
jaded church steps
gel pens and soiled paper scraps
singlets and solitary supplicants
tithes in and tithes back
low sodium split pea cans

take this: sun bleached solitude
bread loaf molded sticky sweet pale
pink candies and
a subdued offering
tithes in and tithes back
butter pats sun drenched
lonesome collections ten percent
of what I have I tithe back

of creep slow genuflect
of how god's love it bestows
a bruised green apple and cracker jacks
church steps hunchback
of what I have I tithe back
of the Lord's love like so: tender glows
tender glow

a bee on the Brooklyn bound N
(the throat closes)

this is the exhilaration of life
out of place, an animal heartbeat
where there should be none, a sparrow's shrill
call from the airport's eaves
a cockroach lurking
in the cool aseptic corners, a scorpion creeping
in my neat dresser drawer, a disemboweled
field mouse on the dining room floor,
bones broken like pine
needles, headless
mouth agape in supplication, splayed
this is the exhilaration of life
out of place

we each have a decision to make
alto drone at our ankles, never seen this
kind of lone bee life swiping its own
metrocard, boarding the train at dusk with us
she preys then crushes, moment of silence
a little life in an open casket,
its wings so radiant and listless, a dirge
I feel sick in the same way as when I see
maggots feasting, decadent
each passenger with her own disbelief
at the end of a life out of place
she must have been stung before

she must be protecting her newborn
she spent years trying for
or maybe she just can't stand
the sight of life out of place

multiple times over the years
I've liberated sparrows
who've found their way indoors
atop my dinner table
arbiters of a keen wild and
a coming liberation
when I trap them in a dish towel
releasing them, bright eyed and feral
freeing them in the release

████, always

I.

This morning my ████
trimmed the only red geranium
and placed it on the kitchen table
where I would surely see.
that's because he loves me
unconditionally.

II.

This morning my ████
trimmed the only red geranium
and placed it on the kitchen table
where I would surely see.
that's because he loves me
and knows that darkness creeps.

III.

This morning my ████
trimmed the only red geranium
and placed it on the kitchen table
where I would surely see.
that's because he loves me
dutifully

IV.

This morning my ███████
trimmed the only red geranium
and placed it on the kitchen table
where I would surely see.
that's because he loves me
enough to set me free

V.

This morning, my ████████
yesterday's dusk, my ████████
standard time sunrise, my ███████.
my ████████ packed a little
knapsack and kissed me on the forehead.
tonight the big bed is mine
I invite the darkness.

this is a library

this is a library
these are books
this is men with nowhere to go
this is the Chelsea Hotel
these are pee boots
this is a keen stench
these are letters
this is the mystery collection
and this is a library
this is a respite
this is a heads down hotel
this is a man doing his job
tap tap on the shoulder
this is no motel
this is a toilet flushing loudly
this is a potent stench
this is the greasiest hair
these are bent backs
this is everyone there everyone
alone this is old men no sons
this is some love then none
this is hot hope done gone
this is a hot weather respite
this is a winter shelter
these are books
this is Gwendolyn Brooks
these are the weathered books

these are the weathered men
this is a lit lantern an ancient
hope a queuing disaster
this is a library
rainy day and wet dog men
5 PM lights out
the men return tomorrow
no doubt
no doubt

textures of a waning summer

what these sweet joys and unfettered troubles
school children ebullient
all the light is a crowned crystal
at the break of the morn
all six these children singing the exact same song
everyone's uniforms still crisp barely worn
teenagers and children born

laggards toss Cheetos bags at the tree wells and
gutters and summer is nearly over if not for
all six these ones singing
in crisp, prophetic unison
the smallest one on bike pegs
the biggest one with beanstalk legs

a gestation of 77 days

what harpoons this stark
unlikely life, hurtling into the
light with life meets light?
what calming chasm chaos
in a knapsack? what little girl blue
nursing at my breast? what creamy
animal creature claiming me as
her mother? what yearning life
leeching, shackled together?

now this body's forgetting, this
accounting for old but also healing, this
keloid scar tissue over new fissures, this
chapel racked, this ruin this drifting

a reprieve in the body's question
rhetorical, fractures gestures and scars
and no teeny infant in the new year.
to be clear: the body's sojourned

at twenty-four weeks this is what
would have been: skinny turtle legs
and cognitive function, at twenty-four
weeks you can birth your kin, at
twenty-four weeks there's this: brethren,
body, mountain, infant
peak, valley, oh volatile shore

break the day as we break bones
cast a light to this luminous sun
cast a net to the slick, shallow edges
beat back beat black a molten blood
curry a thickest heat down on our
knees and come whitest light for
the teeming life bound to come. come
light, for the teeming life when it does

Untitled #3/ vespers

A slim Strait is my new religion the homily a clean clear palm
its imprint reflecting in the sun

clean heart

I took the world with a clean heart I took the world
with my dog he searched out chicken bones and
stench and searched for them on his own

your mind is bright and wild as a snail's
your mind is a slow burn
your mind is bright and wild as a snail's
and you long for the April Ohio hail
yeah
for the April Ohio hail
I sent my love out in a fishing boat
expecting she'd return
I knew there to be hail salt water
but her good mind always comes home
yeah
but her good mind always comes home

I look to the east and a search the west
for the best the sea can give
I know it's full of mollusks and scallops
and young birds that are waiting for a home
for new birds who need good homes

our young green hearts beat red
our young new hearts beat red
a full bottle of solid waters and
our ship's setting sail tomorrow
and our ship's setting sail tomorrow

Peter Late Eulogy
(a throat opens)

I invite you to mourn, finally, for Peter that breezy August '94, to break bread at the grave, breathe in some of Peter: knobby knees nearsighted multivariate calculus monsignors and fathers a little brother we all adore.

I rummage hope and hopeless, tidy widower's room tomes in languages I've yet to know and you walk in the slick near edges alone. Myself at twelve: skinned knee, bleach–clean, inculpable. Peter, sixteen, our ascendant progeny, Peter the rock your body

A swan dive assured, such gravity. Peter, I think in you and invite you to mourn, finally. A litany is a stark plain, a cleansing newness, a buffered passage, a litany is a low tide, a heat embalmed by wolves aeternam and you are just one.

Peter ancient animal, your best kin bygone. At sixteen every deadbeat is a fresh wound, every shoulder is a slick sucker. And I atone. Please speak, your voice I cannot remember. Peter, do you know your father is finally proud and Peter, would you believe how the Eucharist, incense, clemency and scorn can choke a requiem?

We sit silent for Peter. We all succumb, a dirge this dearth this asteroid light can you imagine such finality? Peter walks from Silver Spring to Gaithersburg low hanging oak leaves at his bird neck, a whisperer a whisper he walks slick near the edges, I invite you to shelter.

This house should hold a new prayer or this house should burn. We should sit with Peter when the darkness breaches. I wonder about your vices I don't know of your malice I wonder if a life creeps in your womb and if maggots feast in your womb I wonder if your brother visits I wonder who thinks in you I wonder if when we'll regard the truth. The truth is you are untamed and boundless, big for that small house of reticent Catholics, a sunlit garret in the darkness Peter we keep you.

Peter this is the only thing I really remember: you staring directly into the sun your face contorted, wild, no one understood you were laughing, finally. I see in you when I search for what made that place holy, when I want to know the truth. We can finally see you. You need to rest in peace. To the breaking bread at your grave you write our new prayers. For all souls' pillage in remembrance as a boy in a shroud and a pasture to the night.

children 2002

we were children when we met
the buoyant salts of the sea
licking at us our necks
caking us in crystalline sheets
a saline map of the body's
geography charts security
coarse salt preserves us as
ravenous needy
cryogenic carcasses

at age twenty we split words
summon hope incant gods
spit love
lick lap
yearn

we cornered the sun
those days were infinite
our only clothes caked deep
with the desert's particles: sands
earth-matte clays staining our
nail beds, seashells prickly pear
pomegranates ravenous
and racked by
a capacious need, thirst
quenched by lapping
straight from the sea

we feast on everything, cannibalizing a
boundless desire to know everything
feral greedy anemic animal

the days abut each other in a limitless
autumn, a cavity filled only by
god, truth, thrill, you, in that order
a salted carcass preserves a certain youth
salt preserves the truth

we three

I close my eyes I remember a body of water, you've heard of it, it's the Mediterranean. I remember it from a few angles, always angling for new angles, though, wanting to see it from a lot of different vantages, wanting to smell its north south east and west animal mistral winds, storms, salt flats, hillside stepped vineyards, heat, stars, travelers. Today my sister taught me how to float. Now, I am squinting straight into the sun and no one is there except we three. We three are a small nation, all eyes closing and a peace so peaceful and a water so still and waveless beckoning what's reckless as it washes over our forearms. I'm not sinking, I'm floating. We're all bobbing creatures amniotic salted on this island of deserted windmills. No one has even thought about the children at all. The children don't care much if they are burning under the sun, at least not for this moment.

other bodies of water

I think back to the water's flawless underside, deep within the thickets that are heavy with the summer is rich with moss and wild raspberries as I trace our old mill town on a map to know keenly the days: that is where we harvested elderberries. That's where we stepped gingerly over shards of glass. That's where you taste metallic. That's where I remember you know me. That's where we were reminded, that's where we remained. That's where we made vaults of our stories.

The River Cervo rises in its sweet acridity, we know a few bodies of water. That's where I watched you from the keyhole. I let my weight meet yours, you have three dimples; I can count them we are flung asunder and afield. I have a lot I need to tell you.

a dinghy

for the crystalline sea, festooned
and Ronda's neat searing crevasse
succumbed
a squid's inky family
and for you, a sharp fold
that says it's the sun

Notes

home 16 ways

- Matthew Cassel. *The Journey*. May 23, 2016. *The New Yorker*.
- For the concept of a country as a wayward brother you always love: "It's like a gangster big brother, you love him anyway". Bona Park. 2009. Biella, Italy.

Lida meet lorry/ after Parndorf

- *A Day After 71 Migrants Died, 81 Escaped the Back of a Truck in Austria.* Alison Smale. September 4, 2015. *New York Times*.
- *Austria's migrant disaster: Why did 71 die?* Bethany Bell & Nick Thorpe. August 25, 2016. *BBC News*.

Some latitude. A crease.

- *Joanna Macy: A Wild Love for the World*. August 11, 2016. *On Being with Krista Tippett*.
- *Widening Circles* as it appeared in *On Being*. August 11, 2016. Rainer Maria Rilke. Translation by Joanna Macy and Anita Barrows.

conversations from empire

- *Mediterranean death toll soars in first 5 months of 2016*. Adrian Edwards and Medea Savary. May 31, 2016. UNHCR. "I am a good swimmer, I've always lived by the sea". As stated by Hamin in this report.
- *Liberation from Concentration Camps: The Complexity of Concluding the Holocaust Narrative*. Nina Kovalenko. Spring 2011. *Primary Source*. Indiana University

collage for Youngbird/ after Malia Wollan's "How To Hold a Heart"

- Malia Wollan. *How to Hold a Heart.* January 8, 2016. *New York Times Magazine.*
- The "bird can feed bird" line is from Amy Lafty, as read aloud in Home School Hudson's Myung Mi Kim's workshop.

Calais, onward

- *The Wetsuitman.* Text: Anders Fjellberg. Photos. Photos: Tomm W. Christiansen & Hampus Lundgren. June/ July 2015. *Magasinet. Dagbladet.*

still life on lesbos

- Sappho, as translated by Anne Carson, for the lines "I would not think to touch the sky with two arms." From *If not, Winter: Fragments of Sappho.* August 12, 2003. Knopf Doubleday Publishing Group.

I. Fittja, Sweden

- *Avoiding Risky Seas, Migrants Reach Europe With an Arctic Bike Ride.* Andrew Higgins. October 9, 2015. *New York Times.*

remember: we, too, are but the fold

- *Stepping Over the Dead on a Migrant Boat.* Rick Gladstone. October 5, 2016. *New York Times.*

young warblers, golden plovers, loons

- The lines "Oh there's the sun I will say, pointing at the moon." is paraphrased from a line in a piece by my friend Heena Shah.

testament, a litany for many voices

- Thanks to Kate Tempest's *Brand New Ancients* for the inspiration for my last three stanzas. *Brand New Ancients* was published on March 10, 2015 by Bloomsbury.

Peter Late Eulogy/ (a throat opens)

- The line "I think in you" comes from Lili Glauber.

All images taken by Asiya Wadud.

Acknowledgements

Thank you always to my English conversation students at the Brooklyn Public Library whose persistent inquiry encourages me to think about language anew.

I wrote this book in 2016. Thank you so many times over to Susie Sokol, Josh Barocas, Kate Savoca and all the Saint Ann's School second graders for what you taught me.

The generosity of the faculty and staff at Home School Hudson 2016: Adam Fitzgerald, Douglas Kearney, Myung Mi Kim, Dorothea Lasky, Harryette Mullen, Tara Geer, Emily Skillings and Saretta Morgan. Also my workshop colleagues, particularly Henk Rossouw and Rachael Wilson.

Tracie Morris, Jason Koo and Brenda Coultas for the new ways to see in each of your workshops. Mona Talbott and Kate Arding: the time at your beautiful home in Hudson, New York and your generosity was exactly what I needed.

Emily Skillings for championing the pieces I wrote during Home School Hudson and helping me find homes for them. Danniel Schoonebeek, Stacy Szymaszek, *The Felt* editors, and *SUBLEVEL* guest editors, Maggie Nelson and Janice Lee, for publishing early work. Matthew Cassel, whose series *The Journey*, set my work on a new course. Bouchra Khalili, for *The Mapping Journey Project*. I return to it often. Okwui Okpokwasili for a clear lineage of body and language.

Ping Zheng, who I met teaching English at the Brooklyn Public Library and whose luminous work graces the cover of *Crosslight for Youngbird*. How lucky that we can work together in so many ways.

Julia Staniszewska for your steady propulsion and insistence. JSJ for all you taught me about the open waters. Lili Glauber for your supple, bright mind and ability to turn the same stone a thousand different ways. My unwavering mother, Salaama Wadud, and my sisters, Imani Wadud and Ibada Wadud, for their deep well of love.

In 2017, Portable Press @ Yo-Yo Labs published the first half of this book as the chapbook, *we, too, are but the fold*. Thank you immensely to Brenda Iijima and Nicholas DeBoer for working with me so closely to create this work.

And finally, to Lindsey Boldt, Kazim Ali, Andrea Abi-Karam, HR Hegnauer, and Stephen Motika for believing in this project and working with me to bring it to life.

Publications

"my little nothings form a mouth." *The Felt*. 2016.

"Calais, onward" and "Jamila." *The Recluse*. 2016.

"conversations from empire." *PEN Poetry Series*. 2016.

"Lida meet lorry." *SUBLEVEL*, Issue #1: CONTAGION. 2017.

we, too, are but the fold. Portable Press @ Yo-Yo Labs. 2017.

"still life on lesbos." *Sixth Finch*. 2017.

"other bodies of water." *Makhzin*, Issue 3: Dictationship. 2018.

ASIYA WADUD is a writer and third grade teacher. She is the author of the chapbook *we, too, are but the fold*. Every Wednesday, she teaches English to new immigrants and refugees. She lives in Brooklyn, New York.

Nightboat Books

Nightboat Books, a nonprofit organization, seeks to develop audiences for writers whose work resists convention and transcends boundaries. We publish books rich with poignancy, intelligence, and risk. Please visit our website, www.nightboat.org, to learn about our titles and how you can support our future publications.

The following individuals have supported the publication of this book. We thank them for their generosity and commitment to the mission of Nightboat Books:

Kazim Ali
Anonymous
Photios Giovanis
Elenor & Thomas Kovachevich
Elizabeth Motika
Leslie Scalapino – O Books Fund
Benjamin Taylor
Jerrie Whitfield & Richard Motika

In addition, this book has been made possible, in part, by grants from the National Endowment for the Arts and New York State Council on the Arts Literature Program.